CALCULUS

CLEP* Test Study Guide

> All rights reserved. This Study Guide, Book and Flashcards are protected under the US Copyright Law. No part of this book or study guide or flashcards may be reproduced, distributed or stored in a retrieval system, or transmitted in any form or by any means, electronic, mechanical, photocopying, recording, or otherwise, without the prior written permission of the publisher Breely Crush Publishing, LLC.

© 2020 Breely Crush Publishing, LLC

*CLEP is a registered trademark of the College Entrance Examination Board which does not endorse this book.

971010420143

Copyright ©2003 - 2020, Breely Crush Publishing, LLC.

All rights reserved.

This Study Guide, Book and Flashcards are protected under the US Copyright Law. No part of this publication may be reproduced, distributed or stored in a retrieval system, or transmitted in any form or by any means, electronic, mechanical, photocopying, recording, or otherwise, without the prior written permission of the publisher Breely Crush Publishing, LLC.

Published by Breely Crush Publishing, LLC
10808 River Front Parkway
South Jordan, UT 84095
www.breelycrushpublishing.com

ISBN-10: 1-61433-627-X
ISBN-13: 978-1-61433-627-3

Printed and bound in the United States of America.

*CLEP is a registered trademark of the College Entrance Examination Board which does not endorse this book.

Table of Contents

Limits 1
   What is a limit? 1
   What is continuity? 1

Differential Calculus 2
   What is a derivative? 2
   How is the definition of a derivative used? 2
   What is the Intermediate Value Theorem? 3
   How do you find the derivative of an elementary function? 4
   How do you find the derivative of a sum (or difference)? 5
   How do you find the derivative of a product of two functions? 5
   How do you find the derivative of a quotient of two functions? 6
   What is the derivative of a composite function? 6
   What does it mean to find the derivative of an implicitly defined function? 7
   How do you find the derivative of the inverse of a function? 8
   What are derivatives of higher order? 9
   What is the relationship between the graphs? 9
   What is the Mean Value Theorem? 9
   What is the relation between differentiability and continuity? 10
   What is De L'Hopital's rule? 10

Applications of the Derivative 11
   How do you find the slope at a point in Calculus? 11
   How do you find tangent lines of a function? 11
   How does linear approximation relate to the tangent line? 11
   How does the velocity and acceleration of a particle moving along a line relate to Calculus? 14
   What are average and instantaneous rates of change? 15
   What are related rates of change? 15

Integral Calculus 16
   What are antiderivatives? 16
   Integration through geometry 16
   Integration using Reimann Sums 17
   Left-endpoint approximation 17
   Right-endpoint approximation 18
   Middle approximation 18
   What is an example of basic integration? 19

What are primitive and indefinite integrals?..*20*
What is integration by u-substitution? *21*
When would you use integration by u-substitution? *21*
What are some applications of antiderivatives? *22*
What is a Definite Integral? *23*
What is the Fundamental Theorem of Calculus? *25*
Mean Value Theorem (Integrals)..*25*

Solids of Rotation..*26*
   What are solids of rotation? *26*
   Disc Method *26*
   Washer Method..*27*

Sample Test Questions...*28*
Answer Key *65*
Test-Taking Strategies *66*
What Your Score Means *66*
Test Preparation *67*
Legal Note *67*

 # Limits

(5% of Exam)

What is a limit?
If f is a function then $\lim_{x \to a} f(x)$ if and only if, for any chosen positive number, δ, however small, there exists a positive number, δ such that, whenever $0 < |x-a| < \delta$, then $|f(x) - A| < \delta$.

Following are properties of limits:

Limit of a constant: If $f(x) = c$, a constant, then $\lim_{x \to a} f(x) = c$

Limit of a sum or difference: $\lim_{x \to a} [f(x) \pm g(x)] = \lim_{x \to a} f(x) \pm \lim_{x \to a} g(x) = A \pm B$

Limit of a product: $\lim_{x \to a} [f(x) \cdot g(x)] = \lim_{x \to a} f(x) \cdot \lim_{x \to a} g(x) = A \cdot B$

Limit of a quotient: $\lim_{x \to a} \frac{f(x)}{g(x)} = \frac{\lim f(x)}{\lim g(x)} = \frac{A}{B}$ (Note: $B \neq 0$)

Limits that involve infinity:
$\lim_{x \to 0} \frac{1}{x} = \infty$ (This means that as x approaches zero, the value of 1/x approaches infinity. For example $1/0.001 = 1,000$ and $1/0.000001 = 1,000,000$)

Example Limit Problem: Find the limit of $\lim_{x \to 1} f(x) = \lim(3x^2 + x - 2)$.

To solve this problem, you need to know what x value to plug into the function. The problem gives $x \to 1$ so plug in 1 for x.

$(3x^2 + x - 2)$
$(3(1^2) + 1 - 2) = 2$

Therefore, the limit = 2.

What is continuity?
A function $f(x)$ is continuous if it is continuous at every point of its domain. Basically, a continuous function is one where the following three conditions hold:

1) $f(a)$ exists

2) $\lim_{x \to a} f(x)$ exists

3) $\lim_{x \to a} f(x) = f(a)$

An example of a continuous function is $f(x) = x + 1$. You can plug in any value of x and always satisfy the three conditions.

An example of a discontinuous function is $f(x) = \dfrac{1}{x-2}$. The reason is that if you plug in x = 2 it yields 1/0 which is undefined.

Differential Calculus

(55% of Exam)

What is a derivative?
A derivative of a function represents the rate of change of the function. It is the $\dfrac{\text{change in y}}{\text{change in x}}$.

Formally, the derivative is denoted by:

$$f'(a) = \lim_{x \to a} \frac{f(x) - f(a)}{x - a} \quad \text{and} \quad f'(x) = \lim_{h \to 0} \frac{f(x+h) - f(x)}{h}$$

*NOTE: The notation for the derivative of a function can be written in several formats including:

$$f'(x) \text{ and } \frac{du}{dx}.$$

How is the definition of a derivative used? Derivatives, or the slope of the line at a point, can be found using this definition. Essentially what the definition describes is that as the base of a Reimann sums approximation becomes smaller and smaller (i.e., as the limit of the width of the base approaches zero), the area approximated becomes more exact. This is what an integral is – the exact area under the curve.

Example: Find the derivative of $x^2 + 2x + 1$ using the definition of a derivative.

Answer: The definition of the derivative is as follows. To use it in finding the derivative of a function we must plug in the function, and find the limit. To do this we have to manipulate the equation so that "h" is not alone on the bottom of the equation because that results in an undefined value.

$$f'(x) = \lim_{h \to 0} \frac{f(x+h) - f(x)}{h}$$

$$= \lim_{h \to 0} \frac{(x+h)^2 + 2(x+h) + 1 - (x^2 + 2x + 1)}{h}$$

$$= \lim_{h \to 0} \frac{x^2 + 2xh + h^2 + 2x + 2h - x^2 - 2x}{h}$$

$$= \lim_{h \to 0} \frac{2xh + h^2 + 2h}{h}$$

$$= \lim_{h \to 0} 2x + h + 2$$

$$= 2x + 2$$

Therefore, the derivative of $f(x)$ is: $f'(x) = 2x + 2$.

What is the Intermediate Value Theorem? The Intermediate Value Theorem (IVT) is one of the most base applications of the derivative in calculus. In plain terms, the IVT states that if you have two endpoints at different y values, every value in between must be crossed at some point on that interval. This is demonstrated more formally on the following diagram.

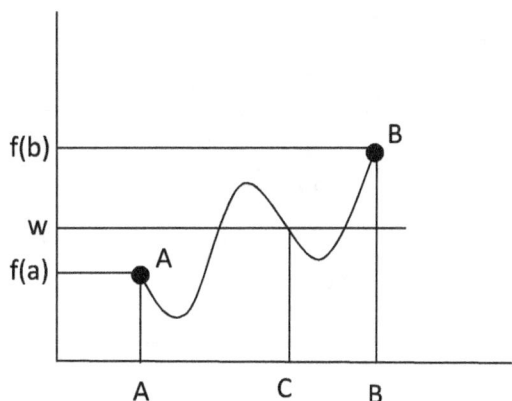

Note: There are three important conditions which must be met for the Intermediate Value Theorem to apply:

1. The line must be a function.
2. The function must be continuous
3. The line must be on a CLOSED interval [a,b].

There must be at least one value C within [A,B] for which $f(C) = w$.

How do you find the derivative of an elementary function? Following is a table of elementary functions and their derivatives. You will need to memorize these.

Function	Derivative
x^n (where n is a natural number)	$\frac{d}{dx}[x^n] = nx^{n-1}$
e^x	$\frac{d}{dx}[e^x] = e^x$
a^x	$\frac{d}{dx}[a^x] = a^x \cdot \ln a$
$\ln x$	$\frac{d}{dx}[\ln x] = \frac{1}{x}$
$\log_a x$	$\frac{d}{dx}[\log_a x] = \frac{1}{x \cdot \ln a}$
x^x	$\frac{d}{dx}[x^x] = x^x \cdot (\ln x + 1)$
$\sin x$	$\frac{d}{dx}[\sin x] = \cos x$
$\cos x$	$\frac{d}{dx}[\cos x] = -\sin x$
$\tan x$	$\frac{d}{dx}[\tan x] = \frac{1}{\cos^2 x}$
$\cot x$	$\frac{d}{dx}[\cot x] = -\frac{1}{\sin^2 x}$

arcsin x	$\frac{d}{dx}[\arcsin x] = \frac{1}{\sqrt{1-x^2}}$
arccos x	$\frac{d}{dx}[\arccos x] = -\frac{1}{\sqrt{1-x^2}}$
arctan x	$\frac{d}{dx}[\arctan x] = \frac{1}{1+x^2}$
arccot x	$\frac{d}{dx}[\text{arccot}\, x] = -\frac{1}{1+x^2}$

How do you find the derivative of a sum (or difference)? For example, find the derivative, $f'(x)$, of $f(x) = x^2 + 4$.

Finding the derivative of $f(x)$ means you have to find $f'(x)$.

Look at each term in the function separately. Multiply the exponent by the coefficient of the variable to find the new coefficient. Then subtract one from the exponent to find the new exponent.

For example: x^2 The original coefficient is 1 and the original exponent is 2.
Multiply 2 × 1 to find the new coefficient of 2.
Subtract 1 from the original exponent of 2 to find a new exponent of 1.
Therefore, the derivative of x^2 is $2x^1$ or just $2x$.

Look at the next term in the function. It is a constant. The derivative of a constant is always zero so that term is dropped completely.

The final answer is $f'(x) = 2x$.

Another example: Find the derivative of $f(x) = 5x^4 + 10x^3 - 6x + 2$.
Answer: $f'(x) = 20x^3 + 30x^2 - 6$

How do you find the derivative of a product of two functions, $f(x)$ and $g(x)$? You differentiate using the Product Rule: $D\{f(x)g(x)\} = f(x)g'(x) + f'(x)g(x)$

Example #1: Differentiate $y = (x^3 + 5x^2 + 2)(3x - 10)$

$$y' = (x^3 + 5x^2 + 2)(3) + (3x^2 + 10x)(3x - 10)$$
$$y' = 3x^3 + 15x^2 + 6 + 9x^3 - 30x^2 + 30x^2 - 100x$$
$$y' = 12x^3 + 15x^2 - 100x + 6$$

Example #2: Differentiate $y = \sin x \cos x$.
$$y' = \sin x(-\sin x) + \cos x(\cos x)$$
$$y' = -\sin^2 x + \cos^2 x$$

How do you find the derivative of a quotient of two functions, $f(x)$ and $g(x)$? You differentiate using the Quotient Rule: $D\{\frac{f(x)}{g(x)}\} = \frac{g(x)f'(x) - f(x)g'(x)}{\{g(x)\}^2}$.

Example #1: Differentiate $y = \frac{2}{x+1}$.
$$y' = \frac{(x+1)(0) - (2)(1)}{(x+1)^2} = \frac{-2}{(x+1)^2}$$

Example #2: $y = \frac{4\sin x}{2x + \cos x}$
$$y' = \frac{(2x + \cos x)(4\cos x) - (4\sin x)(2 - \sin x)}{(2x + \cos x)^2} = \frac{8(x\cos x - \sin x) + 4(\cos^2 x + \sin^2 x)}{(2x + \cos x)^2}$$

Note: $\cos^2 x + \sin^2 x = 1$ (This is a Trigonometry identity)

Therefore, the final answer is:
$$y' = \frac{8(x\cos x - \sin x) + 4(1)}{(2x + \cos x)^2} = \frac{8(x\cos x - \sin x) + 4}{(2x + \cos x)^2}$$

What is the derivative of a composite function, $h(x) = f(g(x))$? You differentiate composite functions using the Chain Rule: $h'(x) = f'(g(x)) \cdot g'(x)$.

Example #1: Differentiate $y = (3x+1)^2$.
To answer this problem first differentiate the outside "square" leaving the $(3x + 1)$ unchanged. Then differentiate the inside $(3x + 1)$.

Answer:
$y' = 2(3x+1)^{2-1}(3)$
$y' = 6(3x+1)$

Example #2: Differentiate $y = (5x^3 - 10x^2 + 4)^4$
Answer: $y' = 4(5x^3 - 10x^2 + 4)^3(15x^2 - 20x)$

Example #3: Differentiate $y = \sin(x^3 + \tan(x))$
Answer: $y' = \cos(x^3 + \tan(x))(3x^2 + \sec^2(x))$

Example #4: Differentiate $y = \ln(3x^2 + 9x + 4)$

Answer: $y' = \dfrac{1}{3x^2 + 9x + 4} \cdot (6x + 9) = \dfrac{6x + 9}{3x^2 + 9x + 4}$

Example #5: Differentiate $y = 3e^{(x^2 - 4)}$

Answer: $y' = 3e^{x^2 - 4} \cdot 2x = 6xe^{x^2 - 4}$

What does it mean to find the derivative of an implicitly defined function?
Derivatives of implicitly defined functions can be found using a special case of the Chain Rule.

An example of an implicit function is an equation for the circle such as $x^2 + y^2 = 25$.

Example #1: To find the derivative of $x^2 + y^2 = 25$, first write the derivative in EXPLICIT terms. You can change the function into EXPLICIT terms by solving for y.

Therefore,
$x^2 + y^2 = 25$
$y^2 = 25 - x^2$
$y = \pm\sqrt{25 - x^2}$ or $\pm(25 - x^2)^{\frac{1}{2}}$

NOTE: $y = +\sqrt{25 - x^2}$ represents the top half of the circle while $y = -\sqrt{25 - x^2}$ represents the bottom half of the circle.

So if $y = +\sqrt{25-x^2} = (25-x^2)^{\frac{1}{2}}$ then

$$y' = \frac{1}{2}(25-x^2)^{\frac{-1}{2}}(-2x) = \frac{-x}{\sqrt{25-x^2}}.$$

Example #2: Differentiate $x^3 + y^3 = 4$. It is important to note that you don't always have to write the function explicitly as we did in Example #1. Instead, you can differentiate both sides of the equation separately and then solve for y'.

Answer: Differentiate both sides separately gives $3x^2 + 3y^2y' = 0$.

NOTE: You need multiply the y term by y' because you are differentiating with respect to y.
$3x^2 + 3y^2 y' = 0$
$3y^2 y' = -3x^2$
$y' = \frac{-3x^2}{3y^2} = \frac{-x^2}{y^2}$

How do you find the derivative of the inverse of a function? Let $f(x)$ be an invertible function, with $f^{-1}(x)$ as its inverse. In other words, $f \bullet f^{-1}(x) = x$ and $f^{-1} \bullet f(x) = x$.

Example #1: Let $f(x) = \tan(x)$. The inverse of this function is $f^{-1}(x) = \arctan(x)$. Then find the derivative of $\arctan(x)$.

Answer: $\arctan'(x) = \dfrac{1}{\tan'(\arctan(x))} = \dfrac{1}{1+\tan^2(\arctan(x))}$.

Example #2: Find the derivative of $f(x) = (\arcsin(x))$.

Answer: $f'(x) = \dfrac{1}{\cos(\arcsin(x))}$

Note: $\cos(x) = \sqrt{1-\sin^2(x)}$

Therefore, $f'(x) = \dfrac{1}{\cos(\arcsin(x))} = \dfrac{1}{\sqrt{1-x^2}}$.

What are derivatives of higher order? The derivative of a function $f(x)$ is $f'(x)$ which is called the first derivative. Successive derivatives of $f(x)$ are higher order derivatives. For example, the derivative of $f'(x)$ is $f''(x)$ and so on. Each time you differentiate you will use the same rules of differentiation that you used to find the derivative of the original function.

Example #1: $f''(x)$ of $f(x) = 5x^4 + 2x^3 - 7x^2 + 8x - 2$.

Answer:
$f(x) = 5x^4 + 2x^3 - 7x^2 + 8x - 2$
$f'(x) = 20x^3 + 6x^2 - 14x + 8$
$f''(x) = 60x^2 + 12x - 14$

What is the relationship between the graphs of $f(x), f'(x),$ and $f''(x)$?

Remember the derivative of a function represents the $\frac{\text{change in y}}{\text{change x}}$ which is the slope of a graph.

Therefore, $f'(x)$ represents the slope of $f(x)$. Similarly, $f''(x)$ represents the slope of $f'(x)$. Following is a graphical example where $f(x) = x^2$. The graph of the original function $f(x) = x^2$ is in black. The slope of $f(x) = x^2$ is $2x$ which is the red function the graph. Finally, the slope of $f'(x) = 2x$ is 2. Therefore, $f''(x) = 2$ which is represented by the blue horizontal line at $y = 2$.

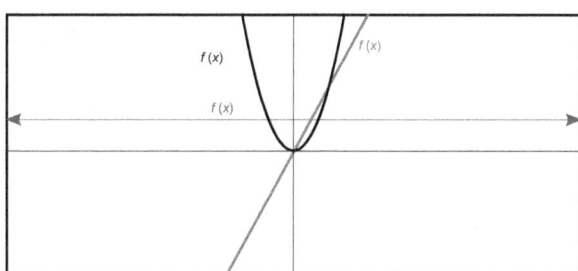

What is the Mean Value Theorem? The Mean Value Theorem states that if $f(x)$ is defined and continuous on the interval $[a,b]$ and differentiable on (a,b), then there is at least one number c in the interval (a,b) such that:

$$f'(c) = \frac{f(b) - f(a)}{b - a}$$

NOTE: The interval (a,b) means the interval $(a < c < b)$.

The Mean Value Theorem states that there exists a point c (a,b), such that the tangent line is parallel to the line passing through $(a, f(a))$ and $(b, f(b))$.

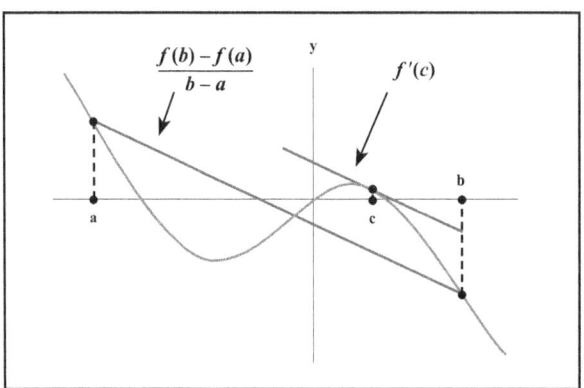

Example #1: Let $f(x) = \dfrac{1}{x}$, where $a = -1$ and $b = 1$.

Answer: $f'(c) = \dfrac{f(b) - f(a)}{b - a} = \dfrac{1 - (-1)}{1 - (-1)} = \dfrac{2}{2} = 1$

What is the relation between differentiability and continuity? If a function is differentiable at some point then it is a continuous function at this point. Also if a function is discontinuous at some point then it has no derivative at this point.

What is De L'Hopital's rule? De L'Hopital's rule is a theorem that says:

Let $x \to a$ for functions $f(x)$ and $g(x)$, differentiable in some neighborhood of the point a, the conditions are executed:

1) either $f(x) \to 0, g(x) \to 0$ or $f(x) \to \infty, g(x) \to \infty$

2) the limit $\lim\limits_{x \to a} \dfrac{f'(x)}{g'(x)}$ exists, then $\lim\limits_{x \to a} \dfrac{f(x)}{g(x)} = \lim\limits_{x \to a} \dfrac{f'(x)}{g'(x)}$.

Basically, De L'Hopital's rule enables you to calculate limits of ratios of functions, when both a numerator and denominator approach either zero or infinity.

Example #1: De L'Hopital's rule says $\lim\limits_{x \to 0} \dfrac{\sin x}{x} = \lim\limits_{x \to 0} \dfrac{\cos x}{1} = 1$.

Example #2: De L'Hopital's rule says $\lim_{x \to 0} \dfrac{\ln x}{1/x} = \lim_{x \to 0} \dfrac{1/x}{-1/x^2} = \lim_{x \to 0} (-x) = 0$.

 Applications of the Derivative

How do you find the slope at a point in Calculus? You need to find derivative of the function at the point. Basically, it is the slope of the tangent line to that graph at the point.

Example #1: Let $f(x) = x^3 - 2x^2 + 4x$ at $(1,3)$.

Answer: Find the derivative and then plug in the point (1,3).
$f'(x) = 3x^2 - 4x + 4$
$f'(1) = 3(1^2) - 4(1) + 4 = 3$

The slope is 3.

How do you find tangent lines of a function? Remember the slope of a line is m. If the derivative of f is m at a point (x_0, y_0) then the point slope equation of the tangent line is $y - y_0 = m(x - x_0)$.

Example #1: Find the tangent line of the $y = 4x^2$ at the point (-1, 4).

Answer:
$y = 4x^2$
$y' = 8x$
$y'(-1) = -8$
$y - 4 = -8(x - (-1))$
$y - 4 = -8x - 8$
$y = -8x - 4$

How does linear approximation relate to the tangent line? The tangent line of $f(x)$ at a point is a linear function that represents the linear approximation of $f(x)$.

What are characteristics of curves when you sketch them? A sketch of a curve (or function) can tell you a great deal about that function. The key is to look at the first and second derivative.

You need to memorize these characteristics of function sketches:
1. If the first derivative f' is positive (+) then the function f is increasing ($\uparrow$).

2. If the first derivative f' is negative (-) then the function f is decreasing ($\downarrow$).

3. If the second derivative f'' is positive (+) then the function f is concave up ($\cup$).

4. If the second derivative f'' is negative (-) then the function f is concave down ($\cap$).

5. The point $x = a$ determines a relative maximum for a function f if f is continuous at $x = a$ and the first derivative f' is positive (+) for $x < a$ and negative (-) for $x > a$. The point $x = a$ determines an absolute maximum for function f if it corresponds to the largest y-value in the range of f.

6. The point $x = a$ determines a relative minimum for function if f is continuous at $x = a$, and the first derivative f' is negative (-) for $x < a$ and positive (+) for $x > a$. The point $x = a$ determines an absolute minimum for function f if it corresponds to the smallest y-value in the range of f.

7. The point $x = a$ determines an inflection point for function f if f is continuous at $x = a$, and the second derivative f'' is negative (-) for $x < a$ and positive (+) for $x > a$, or if f'' is positive (+) for $x < a$ and negative (-) for $x > a$.

8. The Second Derivative Test for Extrema: If $f''(c) < 0$ then f has a relative maximum value at $x = c$. If $f''(c) > 0$ then f has a relative minimum value at $x = c$. If $f''(c) = 0$, then we don't know what is happening at c.

9. A point of inflection on a curve $y = f(x)$ is a point at which concavity changes.

Example #1: Show that $f(x) = x^5 + 20x - 6$ is an increasing function for all values of x.

Answer: Step #1: Find $f'(x)$. $f'(x) = 5x^4 + 20$.
Step #2: Determine whether $f'(x)$ is positive or negative for all values of x. $f'(x)$ is positive for all values of x.

Step #3: Therefore, $f(x) = x^5 + 20x - 6$ is an increasing function for all values of x.

Example #2: Show where the function $f(x) = x^2 + 6x - 11$ increases or decreases.

Answer: $f'(x) = 2x + 6$ therefore the function is decreasing on $(-\infty, -3)$ and increasing on $(-3, +\infty)$. This can be found by setting $f'(x) = 0$ and solving to find that $x = -3$. Because $f'(0) > 0$ and $y'(-4) < 0$, the function is increasing and decreasing in these areas respectively.

Note: $x = -3$ is both a relative and absolute minimum of the equation $f(x)$.

Example #3: Find the absolute maximum and minimum of
$f(x) = x^3 - x^2 - x + 2$ on $[0,2]$.

Step #1: Find the first derivative. $f'(x) = 3x^2 - 2x - 1$.
Step #2: Solve for x to find the critical numbers.
$$f'(x) = 3x^2 - 2x - 1$$
$$f'(x) = (3x + 1)(x - 1)$$
$$x = -\frac{1}{3} \text{ and } 1$$

Step #4: Check to see if the critical x values lie in $[0, 2]$. $x = 1$ lies in $[0, 2]$.
Step #5: 2 is the biggest number in the interval so plug 2 into the original function to find the absolute maximum.
$$f(x) = x^3 - x^2 - x + 2$$
$$f(2) = 2^3 - 2^2 - 2 + 2 = 4$$

Step #6: 0 is the smallest number in the interval so plug 1 into the original function to find the absolute minimum.
$$f(x) = x^3 - x^2 - x + 2$$
$$f(1) = 1^3 - 1^2 - 1 + 2 = 1$$

Example #4: Find the relative extrema of the function $f(x) = x(12 - 2x)^2$.

Answer: Use the Second Derivative Test.
$$f'(x) = x(2)(12 - x)^1(-2) + (12 - 2x)^2 = (12 - 2x)(12 - 6x) = 12(x - 6)(x - 2)$$
$$x = 2, 6$$

Therefore, the critical numbers are x = 2, and x = 6.
$$f''(x) = 12(2x - 8) = 24(x - 4)$$
$$f''(2) = -48$$
$$f''(6) = 48$$

Therefore, f has a relative maximum at $x = 2$ because $f''(2) = -48 < 0$.
f has a relative maximum at $f''(6) = 48 > 0$ because $f''(6) = 48 > 0$.

Example #5: Find the inflection point for the function $f(x) = x^3$.

Answer:
Step #1: Find $f''(x)$.
$f''(x) = 6x$
Solve for x to find the critical numbers. $x = 0$ is a critical number.
Step #2: Determine the sign (+ or -) for $x < 0$ and $x > 0$.
$f''(x) < 0$ and $f''(x) > 0$ for $x = 0$
Therefore, the graph has an inflection point at $x = 0$.

Example #6: Examine $y = 3x^4 - 10x^3 - 12x^2 + 12x - 7$.

Answer:
Step #1: $y'' = 36x^2 - 60x - 24 = 12(3x+1)(x-2)$
Step #2: Solve for x to find the critical numbers which are $x = \frac{-1}{3}$ and 2.

Step #3: When $x < \frac{-1}{3}, y'' = +$ and the arc is concave upward.

When $\frac{-1}{3} < x < 2, y'' = -$ and the arc is concave downward.

When $x > 2, y'' = +$ and the arc is concave upward.

How does the velocity and acceleration of a particle moving along a line relate to Calculus? Velocity and acceleration are rates of change based on time. Derivatives represent rates of changes and are used to solve velocity and acceleration problems.

Velocity is another term for speed and is a function of time.
$V = \frac{s}{t}$ where "s" represents the change in distance and "t" represents time.

In general, $V = \frac{dx}{dt}$.

Example #1: Let the following be the equation of a particle moving along a line:
$x(t) = 6t^2 + t + 8$ where x is in meters and t is in seconds.

What is the velocity of the particle after 10 seconds?

Step #1: Find the derivative of $x(t)$. $\dfrac{dx}{dt} = 12t + 1$

Step #2: Plug in $x = 10$ to find the velocity. $\dfrac{dx}{dt} = 12(10) + 1 = 121 m/sec$

Acceleration, $a(t)$, can be found by taking the derivative of the velocity. Essentially, acceleration is $x''(t)$.

Example #2: What is the acceleration for any time t from Example #1?
Step #1: Find $x''(t)$. $x''(t) = 12$.

Therefore, the acceleration is $12 m/sec^2$.
Note: The units for acceleration are $m/(sec)(sec)$ which is m/sec^2

What are average and instantaneous rates of change? $\dfrac{x'-x}{\Delta t}$ represents the average rate of change between two points x and x'.

The instantaneous rate of change is the rate of change at a specific point. It is the limit of the average velocity, $\dfrac{dx}{dt}$, as dt approaches 0.

What are related rates of change? Related rates of change deal with two parameters that affect each other.

For example, if the radius of a circle is expanding, the diameter of the circle is also expanding.

Example #1: If the radius of a circle is expanding at the rate of $2cm/min$, how fast is the area expanding when the radius is $15cm$?

Answer: We are given $\dfrac{dr}{dt} = 2cm/min$. We also know that $A = 2\pi r$ and $\dfrac{dA}{dt} = 2\pi r \dfrac{dr}{dt}$. Note: This is found through implicit differentiation.

Therefore, when r = 15cm, $\dfrac{dA}{dt} = 2\pi \bullet 15 \bullet 2 = 60\pi$

Integral Calculus

(40% of the Exam)

What are antiderivatives? Basically, antiderivatives are the opposite of derivatives. To compute an antiderivative you would complete the steps you did for derivatives EXCEPT in REVERSE order. Another term for an antiderivative is an integral. Integrals use the symbol $\int$.

Remember how the derivative of f is denoted by f'? Well, the integral of f' is f.

Conceptually, the easiest way to describe integrals, or antiderivatives, is as the area beneath the curve. As such, the two most straightforward ways to calculate integrals are by using simple geometry and by using an approximation method referred to as Reimann sums.

Integration through geometry: Simple geometric ratios and calculations can be used when all of the equations involved in integration are linear or perfectly geometric. It is done by breaking the graph visually into easy to work with shapes, and summing their areas. This is demonstrated in the example below, which has been subdivided into four geometric areas.

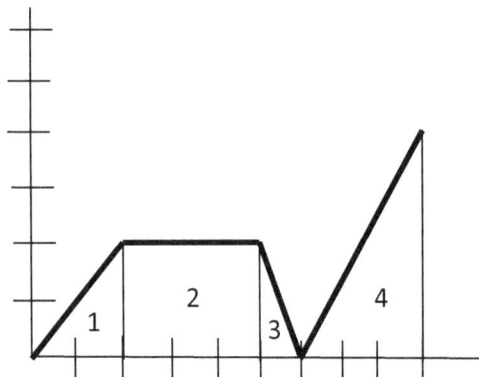

Area 1: A triangle with area (1/2)(base)(height)=(1/2)(2)(2)= 2
Area 2: A rectangle with area (base)(height)=(3)(2)= 6
Area 3: A triangle with area (1/2)(1)(2)=1
Area 4: A triangle with area (1/2)(3)(4)= 6

Therefore, the integral of the function over the given area is the sum of the four areas or 15.

Integration using Reimann Sums: The concept behind Reimann sums is similar to that behind using simple geometry, but using only rectangles. To find the Reimann sums approximation of a function over an interval, you simply have to divided the area into rectangles of a chosen base with the height equal to the height of the line (i.e., the base is x and the height is $f(x)$). Reimann sums can be found using left, right, or center approximations. Each will give a slightly different approximation, so it is important to take note of which is being asked for. Examples are given below. The examples use a base of 2, which means that the areas are divided into four rectangles.

Left-endpoint approximation:

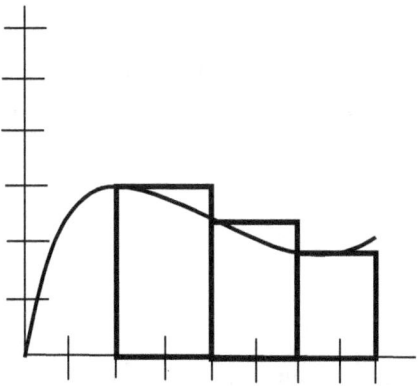

The left endpoint approximation generates the rectangles based on value on the lower or leftmost corner of the rectangle. At this point that makes the heights of the rectangles fall at x = 0, 2, 4, and 6.

Integral = $2(f(0))+2(f(2))+2(f(4))+2(f(6))$
Integral = $2(0)+2(3)+2(2.5)+2(2)$
Integral = $0+6+5+4 = 15$

As you can see, the Reimann sums method is not exact, but it will be more correct as the base widths used become smaller. As is, the left-endpoint method underestimates from x = 0 to x = 2 (where the function is increasing) and overestimates from x = 2 to x = 8 (where the function is decreasing).

Right-endpoint approximation:

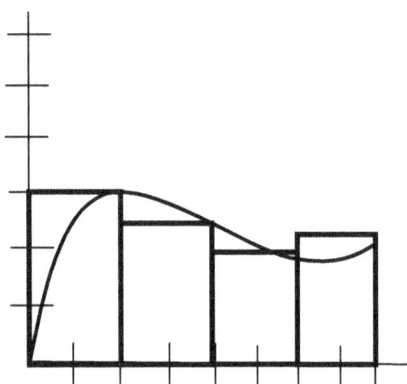

The right-endpoint approximation method draws the rectangles based on the rightmost or higher corner of the rectangle. For this graph this results in the heights of the rectangles falling at x = 2, 4, 6, and 8.

Integral = $2(f(2)) + 2(f(4)) + 2(f(6)) + 2(f(8))$
Integral = $2(3) + 2(2.5) + 2(2) + 2(2.25)$
Integral = $6 + 5 + 4 + 4.5 = 19.5$

As you can see, the right endpoint approximation overestimates from x=0 to x=2, rather than underestimates, and underestimates from x=2 to x=8 rather than overestimates.

Middle approximation:

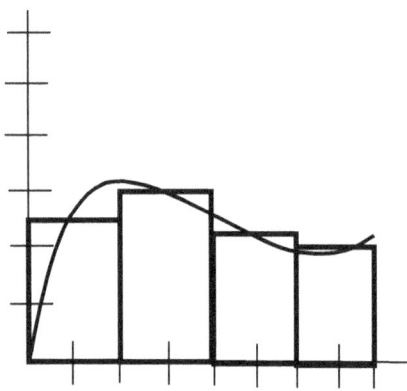

The middle approximation method of Reimann sums is unique because it bases its estimate of height off of the y-value at the center of the base as demonstrated in the figure above. This yields:

Integral = $2(f(1)) + 2(f(3)) + 2(f(5)) + 2(f(7))$
Integral = $2(2.5) + 2(3) + 2(2.5) + 2(2)$
Integral = $5 + 6 + 5 + 4 = 20$

What is an example of basic integration? Integrate $f(x) = 2x^2$.

Look at each term separately. Add one to the exponent to obtain the new exponent. Divide the coefficient by the new exponent. Add the constant C. C is known as the constant of integration.

So, integration of $f(x) = 2x^2$ means $\int 2x^2 = \frac{2}{3}x^3 + C$.

You can check your answer by its derivative. The derivative should be the same as the original function. The derivative of $\frac{2}{3}x^3 + C$ is $2x^2$ so the answer is correct.

Example #1: Integrate $f(x) = 2x^5$.

Answer: $\int 2x^5 = \frac{2}{6}x^6 = \frac{1}{3}x^6 + C$

Example #2: Find the $\int 4$ with respect to x.

Answer: $4x + C$. The integral of a constant can be obtained easily by multiplying it by the variable. Double check your answer. The derivative of $4x$ is 4 so you have found the integral correctly.

Example #3: Compute $\int 4x^{10} - 3x^4 + 2x - 11 \, dx$ Note: The dx means you integrate with respect to x.

Answer: $\frac{4}{11}x^{11} - \frac{3}{5}x^5 + x^2 - 11x + C$

Example #4: Compute $\int \frac{2}{3}y^4 + 3y - 2 \, dy$

Answer: $\frac{2}{15}y^5 + \frac{3}{2}y^2 - 2y + C$

Following are basic indefinite integral formulas that you should know:

Integral of….	Is…
$\int x^n dx$	$\dfrac{x^{n+1}}{n+1} + C$ where C is any constant, called a constant of integration.
$\int \dfrac{1}{x} dx$	$\ln|x| + C$
$\int e^x dx$	$e^x + C$
$\int a^x dx$	$\dfrac{a^x}{\ln a} + C$, where a is a constant
$\int \cos x\, dx$	$\sin x + C$
$\int \sin x\, dx$	$-\cos x + C$
$\int \tan x\, dx$	$-\ln|\cos x|$
$\int \cot x\, dx$	$\ln|\sin x|$
$\int k f(x) dx$	$k \int f(x) dx$, where k is a constant
$\int (f(x) \pm g(x)) dx$	$\int f(x) dx \pm \int g(x) dx$

What are primitive and indefinite integrals?

- A continuous function $F(x)$ is called a primitive for a function $f(x)$ on a segment X, if for each x X, $F'(x) = f(x)$.

  For example, the function $F(x) = x^4$ is a primitive for the function $f(x) = 4x^3$.

- The indefinite integral of a function $f(x)$ on a segment X is a set of all primitives.

An indefinite integral is written as $\int f(x) dx = F(x) + C$ where C is any constant called the "constant of integration."

What is integration by u-substitution?
Integration by u-substitution enables you to algebraically simplify the form of the function. Integration by u-substitution is closely related to the chain rule for differentiation.

When would you use integration by u-substitution?
You use integration by u-substitution when it is difficult to recognize the antiderivative of a function.

Example #1: It would be difficult to recognize the antiderivative for $\int (2x+2)e^{x^2+2x+3} dx$.

Answer: Therefore, follow these steps to integrate by u-substitution:
Step #1: Let $u = x^2 + 2x + 3$.
Step #2: Find the derivative of u which is $\frac{du}{dx} = 2x + 2$.
Step #3: Pretend that the differentiation notation $\frac{du}{dx}$ is an arithmetic fraction. Multiply both sides of the previous equation by dx to get $\frac{du}{dx}dx = (2x+2)dx$ or
$du = (2x + 2)dx$.

Step #4: Make substitutions into the original problem, removing all forms of x, which gives…
$$\int (2x+2)e^{x^2+2x+3} dx = \int e^{x^2+2x+3}(2x+2)dx = \int e^u du = e^u + C = e^{x^2+2x+3} + C$$

Example #2: Find $\int \frac{x^2+1}{x^3+3x} dx$ by u-substitution.

Answer: Let $u = x^3 + 3x$. Therefore, $du = (3x^2 + 3)dx = 3(x^2 + 1)dx$ so that $(1/3)du = (x^2 + 1)dx$. Make substitutions into the original problem, removing all forms of x, which gives…
$$\int \frac{1}{u}(1/3)du = (1/3)\int \frac{1}{u} du = (1/3)\ln|u| + C = (1/3)\ln|x^3+3x| + C.$$

Example #3: Find $\int 4\cos(3x)dx$ by u-substitution.

Answer: Let $u = 3x$ so that $du = 3dx$ or $(1/3)du = dx$.

Next substitute into the original problem, replacing all forms of x, which gives...

$$\int 4\cos(3x)dx = \int 4\cos(u)(1/3)du = (4/3)\int \cos u \, du = (4/3)\sin u + C = (4/3)\sin(3x) + C$$

What are some applications of antiderivatives?
Application #1: Distance and velocity from acceleration with initial conditions.
One example of an application of an antiderivative is deriving distance and velocity from acceleration with initial conditions. We discussed velocity and acceleration with respect to derivatives earlier in this study guide. We were given an equation for motion. Velocity was found by finding the derivative of the equation for motion. We then found acceleration by finding the derivative of the velocity equation.

Essentially, we learned that:

If the distance equation is given by $f(t) = 64t - 16t^2$ then
- Velocity is by the equation $f'(t) = 64 - 32t$
- Acceleration is found by the equation $f''(t) = -32$

With Integrals we can find the velocity and/or distance equation if we are given initial conditions.

Therefore,
- The velocity equation is the $\int$ acceleration.
- The distance equation is the $\int$ velocity.

Example #1: A ball is thrown straight up from the ground with an initial acceleration of -32 ft/sec². The equation for velocity is $v = -32t + 64$.

a) When does the ball reach its maximum height?
Answer: The velocity is 0 at the maximum height. Therefore, $0 = -32t + 64$. Solving for t gives t=2. Therefore, the ball reaches its maximum heigt at 2 seconds.

b) When does the ball hit the ground?
Answer: The ball hits the ground when the distance, *s*, is equal to 0. You must first find the distance equation by finding the integral of the velocity equation.
$\int v = -32t + 64$
$s = -16t^2 + 64t$

Then set the distance equation equal to 0 and solve for t.
$$0 = -16t^2 + 64t$$
$$t = 4$$

Therefore, the ball hits the ground when $t = 4$ seconds.

c) What is the velocity of the ball when it hits the ground?
Answer: The velocity equation is given and we already found that the ball hit the ground at $t = 4$ seconds. Take this information and plug it into the velocity equation.
$$v = -32t + 64$$
$$v = -32(4) + 64 = -64 \, ft/sec$$

Application #2: Solutions of $y' = ky$ and applications to growth and decay.
Antiderivatives can be used to solve growth and decay problems.
Assume that a quantity y varies with time and that $y' = ky$.
The integral of $y' = ky$ is the exponential growth and decay equation which is $y = y_0 e^{kt}$
where k is the "growth constant" and y_0 is the initial value.
  If $k > 0$ it means that y grows exponentially.
  If $k < 0$ it means that y decays exponentially.

Example #1: The population of a country is 100 million people. The population is increasing exponentially with a growth constant $k = \ln 2$. What will the population of this country be after 5 years?

Answer: This is an exponential growth problem. Use the $y = y_0 e^{kt}$ equation with $y_0 = 100$ million, $k = \ln 2$ and $t = 5$. Plug these values into the equation to find $y = 3.2$ billion people.

What is a Definite Integral?
Given a function $f(x)$ that is continuous on the interval [a,b] we divide the interval into n subintervals of equal width, Δx, and from each interval choose a point x_i. Then the definite integral of $f(x)$ from a to b is:

$$\int_a^b f(x)dx = \lim_{x \to \infty} f(x_i) \Delta x$$

Note: "a" is the lower limit of the integral and "b" is the upper limit of the integral.

"a" and "b" can be numbers. They add more work when computing the integral. Basically, you compute the integral just like we did earlier in this study guide. Then you plug in the values for "a" and "b".

You can also look at a definite integral graphically. A definite integral is the limit of a sequence of Riemann sums and approximations of rectangles and trapezoids. This is an approximation of the area under the curve in the interval [a,b].

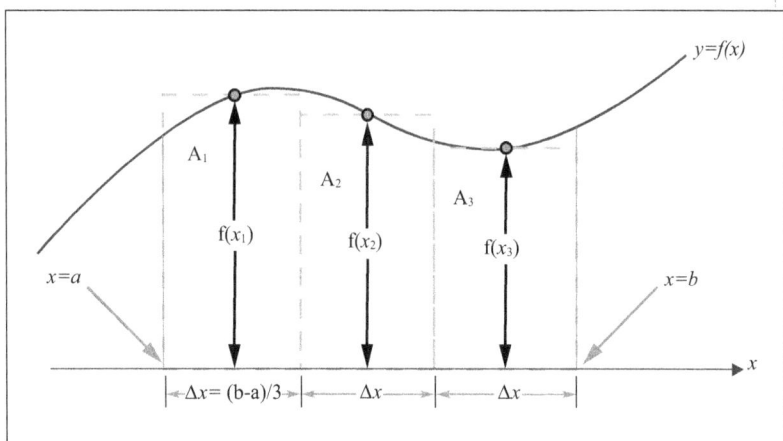

Example #1: Compute $\int_0^2 x^2 + 1 \, dx$.

Answer: $\int_0^2 x^2 + 1 \, dx = \left[\frac{x^3}{3} + x\right]_0^2 = \left[\frac{2^3}{3} + 2\right] - \left[\frac{0^3}{3} + 0\right] = \left[\frac{14}{3}\right] - [0] = \frac{14}{3}$

Example #2: Compute $\int_{-1}^2 (3x^2 - 2x) \, dx$

Answer:
$\int_{-1}^2 (3x^2 - 2x) \, dx = \left[x^3 - x^2\right]_{-1}^2 = \left[2^3 - 2^2\right] - \left[(-1)^3 - (-1)^2\right] = [4] - [-2] = 6$

Example #3: $\int_{-\pi/4}^{\pi/4} \cos 2x \, dx$

Answer: $\int_{-\pi/4}^{\pi/4} \cos 2x \, dx = \left[\frac{1}{2} \sin 2x\right]_{-\pi/4}^{\pi/4} = \frac{1}{2}(1+1) =$

What is the Fundamental Theorem of Calculus?

You have already been using the Fundamental Theorem of Calculus throughout the Integral section of this study guide.

Following is the formal Fundamental Theorem of Calculus:

$$\frac{d}{dx}\int_a^x f(t)dt = f(x)$$

$$\int_a^b F'(x)dx = F(b) - F(a)$$

Tip: Memorize this definition to help you compute Integrals on the exam.

Mean Value Theorem (Integrals)

In calculus, there are actually two different theorems which are referred to as the Mean Value Theorem. The first was mentioned in the derivatives section of this book, and states that at some point the tangent line will be equal to the derivative. The second Mean Value Theorem is relevant to computations using integrals.

Occasionally you will be asked to find the average value of a function over a given area. To do this, simply find the integral over that interval, and divide by the length of the interval. In other words, the average value is equal to

$$\frac{\int_a^b f(x)dx}{b-a}$$

For example, find the average value of the equation between [2,6]. Note: this equation can only be used over a specified CLOSED interval.

Solution: $\dfrac{\int_2^6 x^3 + 2x + 1\, dx}{6-2} = \dfrac{\left[\dfrac{x^4}{4} + 2\right]_2^6}{4} = \dfrac{(326-6)}{4} = 80$

This equation can also be applied in more than just a numerical sense. For example, suppose that it is determined that, based on the amount of predicted rain for the next couple of months, the depth of a certain river at its deepest point will vary according to the equation $f(x) = 50 + 10x - .5x^2$. What will be the average depth of the river at its deepest point over the following 3 months?

Solution: Using the Mean Value Theorem for Integrals, we can determine the average depth of the river as follows:

$$\frac{\int_0^3 50+10x-.5x^2\,dx}{3-0} = \frac{\left[50x+5x^2-.17x^3\right]_0^3}{3} = \frac{190.4}{3} = 63.47 \text{ or about 63 feet.}$$

 ## Solids of Rotation

What are solids of rotation? Integrals can be used to find the area and volume of what are called solids of rotation. These are created by taking a function or shape and rotating it about a line to create a three-dimensional figure. The two methods for finding the volume of a solid of rotation are the disc method and the washer method.

Disc Method: The disc method employs the formula $V = \int_a^b \pi r^2 dr$, where V is volume, [a,b] is the interval defining the shape to be rotated, and r is the radius. When the shape is being rotated around the x axis, or horizontal axis, this means that the formula is $V = \int_a^b \pi f(x)^2 dx$, and when it is being rotated around the y axis, or vertical axis the formula is $V = \int_{f(a)}^{f(b)} \pi f(y)^2 dy$. (Hint: this means that the equation must be in terms of y rather than x as usual.) The disc method is used when a figure is rotated about an axis that boarders it, such as the x or y axis.

Examples using the disc method: Find the volume of $f(x) = x^2$ over the interval [0,2] rotated about the x axis.

Because the disc is rotated about the x axis we leave it in terms of x as it is. Therefore, finding the volume requires only solving the equation given above:

$$V = \int_a^b \pi f(x)^2 dx = \int_0^2 \pi((x^2)^2)dx = \left[\frac{\pi x^5}{5}\right]_0^2 = \frac{32\pi}{5}$$

Example #2: Find the volume of $f(x)=x^2$ over the interval [0,2] rotated about the y axis.

Because the figure is rotated about the y axis you must get the formula in terms of y as follows:

$$f(x) = x^2$$
$$y = x^2$$
$$x = \sqrt{y}$$

To find the bounds of integration we must determine the y values at which x=0 and x=2 fall:

$f(0)=0$
$f(2)=4$

Next, we just plug all of the information into the equation given above and solve it.

$$V = \int_0^4 \pi f(y)^2 dy = \int_0^4 \pi (\sqrt{y})^2 dy = [\pi y]_0^4 = 4\pi$$

Washer method: The washer method is similar to the disc method, but it is used when the axis of rotation does NOT boarder the figure that is being rotated. In other words, this means that there will be a whole in the figure that is being rotated and it will look like a washer (a disc with a whole in it). For example, if the figure being rotated were described by the equation $f(x) = 3x$ bounded by the line $y = 2$ over the interval $[4,6]$, and the figure were being rotated about the x axis.

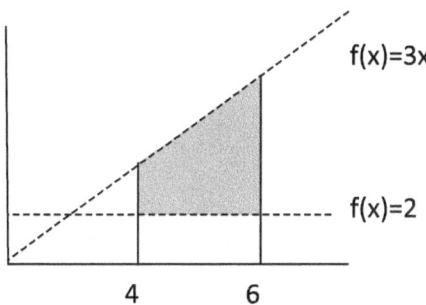

This would create a donut-like shape with a square bottom and slanted top. To find the volume of solids for which this is the case, the equation $V = \pi \int_b^a R^2 - r^2 dr$ where V is the volume, $[a,b]$ is the interval over which the shape is bound (in the example above $a = 4$ and $b = 6$), R is the outer radius of the solid (in the example above $R = 3x$) and r is the inner radius (in the example above $r = 2$).

Hence, the volume of the solid described above would be
$V = \pi \int_4^6 (3x)^2 - 2^2 dx = \pi \int_4^6 9x^2 - 4 dx = \pi [3x^3 - 4x]_4^6 = \pi(624 - 176) = 448\pi$

 ## Sample Test Questions

Limits (5 Questions)

1) Compute $\lim\limits_{x \to 3} \dfrac{5x^2 - 8x - 13}{x^2 - 5}$

Answer: $\lim\limits_{x \to 3} \dfrac{5(3^2) - 8(3) - 13}{(3)^2 - 5} = \dfrac{8}{4} = 2$

2) Compute $\lim\limits_{x \to 0} \dfrac{\sin(5x)}{3x}$

Answer: $\lim\limits_{x \to 0} \dfrac{\sin(5x)}{3x} = \dfrac{0}{0}$. Therefore, apply L'Hopitals rule to find

$\lim\limits_{x \to 0} \dfrac{5\cos(5x)}{3} = \dfrac{5(1)}{3} = \dfrac{5}{3}$

3) Compute $\lim\limits_{x \to -\infty} \dfrac{7}{x^3 - 20}$

Answer: $\lim\limits_{x \to -\infty} \dfrac{7}{x^3 - 20} = \dfrac{7}{-\infty} = 0$. Note: The numerator is always 7 and the denominator $x^3 - 7$ approaches $-\infty$, so that the resulting fraction approaches 0.

4) Compute $\lim\limits_{x \to \infty} \dfrac{100}{x^5 + 5}$

Answer: $\lim\limits_{x \to \infty} \dfrac{100}{x^2 + 5} = \dfrac{100}{\infty} = 0$ Note: The numerator is always 100 and the denominator $x^2 + 5$ approaches ∞ as x approaches ∞, so that the resulting fraction approaches 0.

5) Determine if the following function is continuous at $x = 1$.

$$f(x) = \begin{cases} 3x - 5, & \text{if } x \neq 1 \\ 2, & \text{if } x = 1 \end{cases}$$

Answer: The function is NOT continuous at $x = 1$.

Explanation: Need to satisfy the three conditions for continuity.
1) $f(a)$ exists because $f(1) = 2$. (satisfied)

2) $\lim_{x \to a} f(x)$ exists because $\lim_{x \to a} f(x) = \lim_{x \to a} (3x - 5) = 3(1) - 5 = -2$. (satisfied)

3) However, condition 3 fails because $\lim_{x \to a} f(x) = f(1)$ (not satisfied)

Differential Calculus (55 Questions)

6) What is the derivative of e^x?

Answer: e^x

7) What is the derivative of cos x?

Answer: $-\sin x$

8) What is $f'(x)$ given $f(x) = 8x^3 - 3x^2 + 17x - 40$?

Answer: $f'(x) = 24x - 6x + 17$

9) What is the derivative of arcsin x?

Answer: $\dfrac{1}{\sqrt{1 - x^2}}$

10) What is $\dfrac{d}{dx}[\cot x]$?

Answer: $-\dfrac{1}{\sin^2 x}$

11) What is $f'(x)$ given $y = (x^3 + 7x - 1)(5x + 2)$?

Answer: $y = 20x^3 + 6x^2 + 70x + 9$

Explanation: Use the Product Rule $y'(x) = f(x)g'(x) + f'(x)g(x)$ where $f(x) = (x^3 + 7x - 1)$ and $g(x) = (5x + 2)$.

12) Differentiate $y = x^{-2}(4 + 3x^{-3})$

Answer: $y' = -\dfrac{15 + 8x^3}{x^6}$

Explanation: Use the Product Rule.

13) Differentiate $y = x^3 \ln x$.

Answer: $y' = x^2(1 + 3\ln x)$

Explanation: Use the Product Rule.

$y = x^3 \ln x$
$y' = x^3(\dfrac{1}{x}) + (3x^2)\ln x = x^2 + 3x^2 \ln x = x^2(1 + 3\ln x)$

14) Differentiate $y = 7xe^{x^2}$

Answer: $y' = 7xe^{x^2}(2x + 1)$

Explanation: Use the Product Rule.

$y = 7xe^{x^2}$
$y' = (7x)e^{x^2}(2x) + 7e^{x^2} = 14x^2 e^{x^2} + 7e^{x^2} = 7e^{x^2}(2x^2 + 1)$

15) Differentiate $y = \dfrac{x^2}{3x - 1}$.

Answer: $y' = \dfrac{x(3x - 2)}{(3x - 1)^2}$

Explanation: Use the Quotient Rule.

$$y' = \frac{(3x-1)(2x) - (x^2)(3)}{(3x-1)^2} = \frac{6x^2 - 2x - 3x^2}{(3x-1)^2} = \frac{3x^2 - 2x}{(3x-1)^2} = \frac{x(3x-2)}{(3x-1)^2}$$

16) Differentiate $y = \dfrac{4x^3 - 7x}{5x^2 + 2}$.

Answer: $y' = \dfrac{20x^4 + 59x^2 - 14}{(5x^2 + 2)^2}$

Explanation: Use the Quotient Rule.

17) Differentiate $y = (1 - 4x + 7x^5)^{30}$

Answer: $y' = 30(35x^4 - 4)(1 - 4x + 7x^5)^{29}$

Explanation: Use the Chain Rule. Differentiate the 30th power fist, leaving $(1 - 4x + 7x^5)$ unchanged. Then differentiate $(1 - 4x + 7x^5)$.

18) Differentiate $y = \sqrt{13x^2 - 5x + 8}$.

Answer: $y' = \dfrac{26x - 5}{2\sqrt{13x^2 - 5x + 8}}$.

Explanation: Differentiate the square root first leaving $(13x^2 - 5x + 8)$ unchanged. Then differentiate $(13x^2 - 5x + 8)$.

19) Find $\dfrac{d}{dx} 5\sin(x^2 + 1)$.

Answer: $10x \cos(x^2 + 1)$

Explanation: Use the Chain Rule.
$$\dfrac{d}{dx} 5\sin(x^2 + 1) = 5\cos(x^2 + 1) \cdot 2x = 10x \cos(x^2 + 1)$$

20) Find $\dfrac{d}{dx} \tan(\sqrt{x})$.

Answer: $\dfrac{\sec^2(\sqrt{x})}{2\sqrt{x}}$

Explanation: Use the Chain Rule.
$$\dfrac{d}{dx} \tan(\sqrt{x}) = \sec^2(\sqrt{x}) \cdot \dfrac{1}{2\sqrt{x}} = \dfrac{\sec^2(\sqrt{x})}{2\sqrt{x}}$$

21) Differentiate $f(x) = \sqrt{9x^2 + 4}$.

Answer: $f'(x) = \dfrac{9x}{\sqrt{9x^2 + 4}}$

Explanation: Use the chain rule. Note: $\sqrt{}$ is an exponent of $\dfrac{1}{2}$.

22) Differentiate $f(x) = \sec(9x^2)$.

Answer: $f'(x) = 18x \sec(9x^2) \tan(9x^2)$

Explanation: Use the Chain Rule where:
$f(x) = \sec(x)$ and $f'(x) = \sec(x)\tan(x)$ and $g(x) = 9x^2$ and $g'(x) = 18x$.

23) Differentiate $y = -x^{21} - 3x^{15} - 10x^2 + 105$.

Answer: $y' = -21x^{20} - 45x^{14} - 20x$

24) Differentiate $y = 3x^{\frac{3}{2}} + 2x^{\frac{1}{2}}$.

Answer: $y = \frac{9}{2}x^{\frac{1}{2}} + x^{-\frac{1}{2}} = \frac{9}{2}\sqrt{x} + \frac{1}{\sqrt{x}}$

25) Find $\frac{d}{dx}[\frac{2x+4}{3x-1}]^3$.

Answer: $\frac{-42(2x+4)^2}{(3x-1)^4}$

Explanation: Use the Chain Rule.

$\frac{d}{dx}[\frac{2x+4}{3x-1}]^3 = 3(\frac{2x+4}{3x-1})^2 \cdot \frac{-14}{(3x-1)^2} = \frac{-42(2x+4)^2}{(3x-1)^4}$

26) Find the derivative of $x^2 + y^2 = 16$.

Answer: $\frac{-x}{y}$.

Explanation: Implicit differentiation. Find the derivative of both sides and solve for y'.

$x^2 + y^2 = 16$
$2x + 2y \cdot y' = 0$
$2y \cdot y' = -2x$
$y' = \frac{-2x}{2y} = \frac{-x}{y}$

27) Find the derivative of $x^2 + 6xy + y^2 = 2$.

Answer: $\dfrac{-2x + 6y}{2y + 6x}$

Explanation: Implicit differentiation.

$x^2 + 6xy + y^2 = 2$
$2x + 6x \cdot y' + 6y + 2y \cdot y' = 0$
$6x \cdot y' + 2y \cdot y' = -2x - 6y$
$y'(6x + 2y) = -2x - 6y$
$y' = \dfrac{-2x - 6y}{6x + 2y}$

28) Compute $\dfrac{d}{dx}(\arccos(x))$.

Answer: $-\dfrac{1}{\sqrt{1 - x^2}}$

29) Find the third derivative of $f(x) = 5x^6 + 4x^3 + 8x^2 - 7x + 10$.

Answer: $f'''(x) = 600x^3 + 24$

Explanation:

$f(x) = 5x^6 + 4x^3 + 8x^2 - 7x + 10$
$f'(x) = 30x^5 + 12x^2 + 16x - 7$
$f''(x) = 150x^4 + 24x + 16$
$f'''(x) = 600x^3 + 24$

30) What would the graph look like for the derivative of $f(x) = 3x^2$?

Answer: A straight line with slope 6 and formula $f'(x) = 6x$.

31) What would the graph of f, f', f'' look like for the function $f(x) = 2x^2$? Sketch each function in the space below.

Answer:

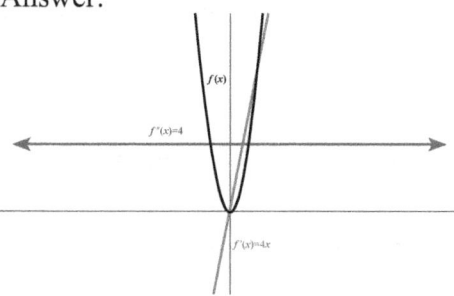

32) Use L'Hopitals Rule to evaluate the following limit.
$$\lim_{x \to 0} \frac{x + \sin 2x}{x - \sin 2x}$$

Answer: -3

Explanation: $\lim_{x \to 0} \frac{x + \sin 2x}{x - \sin 2x} = \frac{1 + 2\cos 2x}{1 - 2\cos 2x} = \frac{1 + 2(1)}{1 - 2(1)} = -3$

33) Where is the function $f(x) = 3x + 5$ increasing and decreasing?

Answer: Increasing everywhere.

34) Where is the function $f(x) = -7x + 20$ increasing and decreasing?

Answer: Decreasing everywhere.

35) Where is the function $f(x) = \sqrt{4 - x^2}$ increasing and decreasing?

Answer: Increasing on (-2,0), decreasing on (0,2)

36) Show that the function $f(x) = 1 - x^3 - x^7$ is a decreasing function for all values of x.

Answer: $f'(x) = -3x^2 - 7x^6$ which is < 0 for all $x \neq 0$. Thus the function is decreasing for all values of x.

37) Locate the absolute maximum or absolute minimum of the function $y = (x - 3)^2$.

Answer: Absolute minimum = (0,3). No absolute maximum.

Explanation: The graph is parabola opening upward with vertex (3,0).

38) Locate the absolute maximum or absolute minimum of the function $y = -x^2$.

Answer: No absolute minimum. Absolute maximum = (0,0).

Explanation: The graph is an parabola opening downward with vertex (0,0).

39) Find the relative extrema for the function $f(x) = x^2 + 2x - 3$.

Answer: $x = -1$ yields a relative minimum -4.

Explanation: Use the first derivative test. Find the derivative. $f'(x) = 2x + 2$. Solve for x from 2(x + 1) = 0 so $x = -1$. Plug $x = -1$ into original function. $f(-1) = (-1^2) + 2(-1) - 3 = -4$.

40) Find the relative extrema for the function $f(x) = (x^2 - 4)^2$.

Answer: $x = 0$ yields a relative maximum 16; $x = \pm 2$ yields relative minimum 0.
Explanation: Use first derivative test.

41) Find the inflection point of the function $f(x) = x^3 + 2x^2 - 4x - 8$

Answer: Inflection point at $x = \dfrac{-2}{3}$.

Explanation: Use the second derivative test.

42) What is the concavity for the function $f(x) = x^2 + 2x - 3$?

Answer: Concave upward everywhere.

Explanation: It is a parabola that opens upwards. Also, $f''(x) = 2$, so it is > 0 or concave upward for all values of x.

43) Determine all the numbers c which satisfy the conclusions of the Mean Value Theorem for the function $f(x) = x^3 + 2x^2 - x$ on $[-1, 2]$.

Answer: $c = \dfrac{-4 \pm \sqrt{76}}{6}$

Explanation: Find the first derivative. $f'(x) = 3x^2 + 4x - 1$. Also plug [-1,2] into the Mean Value Theorem: $f'(c) = \dfrac{f(2) - f(-1)}{2 - (-1)} = \dfrac{14 - 2}{3} = 4$.

Next set $f'(x) = 4$ and solve for c.
$3x^2 + 4x - 1 = 4$
$c = \dfrac{-4 \pm \sqrt{76}}{6}$

44) Find the tangent line of $y = 3x^2$ at the point (2,4).

Answer: $y = 12x - 20$

Explanation: Find the first derivative and use the given point (2,4) write the equation of the tangent line.

$y = 3x^2$
$y' = 6x$
$y'(2) = 6(2) = 12$
$y - 4 = 12(x - 2)$
$y - 4 = 12x - 244$
$y = 12x - 20$

45) Is a function increasing or decreasing if the first derivative of a function is positive?

Answer: Increasing

46) Is a function concave up or concave down if the second derivative is negative?

Answer: Concave down.

47) What is the slope for the function $f(x) = x^3 + 2x^2 + 3$ at (2,4)?

Answer: slope is 20.

Explanation: Find the derivative and plug in $x = 2$.

48) What changes at a point of inflection?

Answer: Concavity

49) What is the derivative of $f(x) = 4$?

Answer: 0

50) What is the derivative of $f(x) = (3x^2 + x + 10)^{-1}$?

Answer: $f'(x) = -(3x^2 + x + 10)^{-2}(6x + 1)$

Explanation: Use the Chain Rule.

51) The position of a falling object is given by the equation $s(t) = 9.8t^2$ where s is in meters and t is in seconds. What is the velocity at the end of 3 seconds?

Answer: $58.8 m/\sec$

Explanation: Velocity $= \dfrac{ds}{dt} = 19.6t = 19.6 \times 3 = 58.8 m/\sec$

52) What is the velocity equation for the motion equation $s(t) = 3t^2$?

Answer: Velocity $= \dfrac{ds}{dt} = 6t$

53) What is the equation for acceleration a at any time t if the equation for motion is $s(t) = 10t^2 - 4t + 8$?

Answer: $a(t) = 20$

Explanation: $a(t) = \dfrac{d^2s}{dt} = 20$

54) What is the acceleration at the end of 3 seconds for $s(t) = 10t^2 - 4t + 8$?

Answer: $a(3) = 20 m/\sec^2$

55) What is the position of a body moving in straight line after 5 seconds for the equation of motion $s(t) = 10t^2 - 4t + 8$ where position is measured in meters?

Answer: $238m$

Explanation: Only need to find position so plug 5 into original equation.
$s(5) = 10(5^2) - 4(5) + 8 = 238m$

56) What is the equation for the velocity v at any time t for the equation of motion $s(t) = 10t^2 - 4t + 8$?

Answer: $v(t) = \dfrac{ds}{dt} = 20t - 4$

Explanation: Find the first derivative to find $v(t)$.

57) What is the velocity v at the end of 5 seconds for $v(t) = \dfrac{ds}{dt} = 20t - 4$?

Answer: 96 m/sec

Explanation: Just plug 5 in for t.

58) If the radius of a circle is expanding at a rate of 4 cm/min, how fast is the area expanding when the radius is 20 cm?

Answer: $160\pi cm^2$ / min

Explanation: $\dfrac{dA}{dt} = 2\pi r \dfrac{dr}{dt}$ so $\dfrac{dA}{dt} = 2\pi \cdot 20 \cdot 4 = 160\pi cm^2$ / min.

59) The volume of a sphere is given by the formula $V = \dfrac{4}{3}\pi r^3$. If r changes with time, how does V change?

Answer: $\dfrac{dV}{dt} = 4\pi r^2 \dfrac{dr}{dt}$

Integral Calculus (40 Questions)

60) Compute $\int (3x^2 - 2x + 3) dx$.

Answer: $\int (3x^2 - 2x + 3) dx = x^3 - x^2 + 3x + C$

Explanation: For each term, add one to the exponent and divide by the new exponent.

61) Compute $\int \sqrt{4 - 2t}\, dt$

Answer: $\int \sqrt{4 - 2t}\, dt = \int (4 - 2t)^{\frac{1}{2}} = \dfrac{-1}{3}(4 - 2t)^{\frac{3}{2}} + C$

Explanation: Chain Rule in reverse.

62) Compute $\int (2-3x)^5 dx$

Answer: $\int (2-3x)^5 dx = \dfrac{-1}{18}(2-3x)^6 + C$

Explanation: Chain Rule in reverse.

63) Compute $\int \cos 3x\, dx$

Answer: $\int \cos 3x\, dx = \dfrac{1}{3}\sin 3x + C$

64) Compute: $\int 4\, dx$

Answer: $\int 4\, dx = 4x + C$

65) Compute: $\int \cos x\, dx$

Answer: $\int \cos x\, dx = \sin x + C$

66) Compute $\int x^6 dx$

Answer: $\int x^6 dx = \dfrac{1}{7}x^7 + C$

67) Compute $\int \dfrac{1}{x^7} dx$

Answer: $\int \dfrac{1}{x^7} dx = \int x^{-7} dx = \dfrac{1}{-6}x^{-6} + C = -\dfrac{1}{6x^6} + C$

68) Compute $\int \sqrt[3]{x}\, dx$

Answer: $\int \sqrt[3]{x}\, dx = \int x^{\frac{1}{3}} dx = \dfrac{1}{4/3} x^{4/3} + C = \dfrac{3}{4}(\sqrt[3]{x})^4 + C$

69) Compute $\int (3x+4)^2 dx$

Answer: $\int (3x+4)^2 dx = \int (9x^2 + 24x + 16)dx = 3x^3 + 12x^2 + 16x + C$

70) Compute $\int \dfrac{x^3 + 5x^2 - 4}{x^2} dx$

Answer:
$\int \dfrac{x^3 + 5x^2 - 4}{x^2} dx = \int (x + 5 - 4x^{-2})dx = \dfrac{1}{2}x^2 + 5x - 4(\dfrac{1}{-1}x^{-1}) + C = \dfrac{1}{2}x^2 + 5x + \dfrac{4}{x} + C$

71) Compute $\int \sin^2 x \cos x \, dx$

Answer: $\int \sin^2 x \cos x \, dx = \int (\sin x)^2 \cos x \, dx = \dfrac{1}{3}(\sin x)^3 + C = \dfrac{1}{3}\sin^3 x + C$

72) Compute $\int x^2 \sqrt{x+1} \, dx$

Answer: $\int x^2 \sqrt{x+1} \, dx = 2(x+1)^{3/2}[\dfrac{1}{7}(x+1)^2 - \dfrac{2}{5}(x+1) + \dfrac{1}{3}] + C$

Explanation: Use substitution. Let $u = x+1$.

73) Compute $\int \dfrac{\cos\sqrt{x}}{\sqrt{x}} dx$

Answer: $2\sin(\sqrt{x}) + C$

Explanation: Use substitution. Let $u = \sqrt{x}$

74) Compute $\int x e^{x^2} dx$

Answer: $\int x e^{x^2} dx = \dfrac{1}{2} e^{x^2} + C$

75) A particle moves along a line with acceleration $2 + 6t$ at time t. What is the velocity of this particle at time t?

Answer: $v(t) = \int a(t)dt = 2t + 3t^2$

76) A particle moves along a line with acceleration $2 + 6t$ at time t. What is the distance equation of this particle at time t?

Answer: $s(t) = \int v(t)dt = t^2 + t^3$

77) If the deceleration of k ft/sec² is needed to bring a particle moving with velocity of 60 ft/sec to a stop in 5 seconds, then $k = $?

Answer: 12 ft/sec²

Explanation: Deceleration (and acceleration) is Velocity/time, 60 ft/sec ÷ 5 sec = 12 ft/sec²

78) A particle starting at rest at $t = 0$ moves along a line so that its acceleration at time t is $12t$ ft/sec². How much distance does the particle cover during the first 3 seconds?

Answer: 54 ft.

Explanation: Plug in $t = 3$ into $a(t) = 12t$ ft/sec²

79) Compute $\int_{-1}^{1}(x^2 - x - 1)dx$

Answer: $\dfrac{-4}{3}$

80) Compute $\displaystyle\int_0^3 \frac{1}{\sqrt{4-x}}dx$

Answer: 2

Explanation: $\displaystyle\int \frac{1}{\sqrt{4-x}}dx = -2\sqrt{4-x}$

$-2\sqrt{4-3} - (-2\sqrt{4-0}) = 2$

81) Compute $\displaystyle\int_2^3 \frac{dy}{2y-3}$

Answer: $\ln\sqrt{3}$

82) Compute $\displaystyle\int_1^2 \frac{3x-1}{3x}dx$

Answer: $1 - \frac{1}{3}\ln 2$

Explanation: Rewrite as $\displaystyle\int_1^2 (1 - \frac{1}{3}\cdot\frac{1}{x})dx = [(x - \frac{1}{3}\ln x)]_1^2 = 2 - \frac{1}{3}\ln 2 - 1 = 1 - \frac{1}{3}\ln 2$

83) Compute $\displaystyle\int_0^1 (2t-1)^3 dt$

Answer: 0

Explanation: Expand the $(2t-1)^3$ first to $(8t^3 - 12t^2 + 6t - 1)$ and then integrate.

84) Compute $\displaystyle\int_0^1 e^{-x} dx$

Answer: $1 - \frac{1}{e}$

85) Compute $\int_1^2 \frac{dz}{3-z}$

Answer: ln 2

Explanation: Evaluate $-\ln(3-z)\big|_1^2$

86) Compute $\int_0^1 xe^{x^2} dx$

Answer: $\frac{1}{2}(e-1)$

Explanation: $\int_0^1 xe^{x^2} dx = \frac{1}{2}e^{x^2}\big|_0^1 = \frac{1}{2}(e-1)$

87) Compute $\int_2^2 x\,dx$

Answer: 0

Explanation: $\int_2^2 x\,dx = \left[\frac{1}{2}x^2\right]_2^2 = 2-2 = 0$ NOTE: Since a = b, the integral = 0.

88) A train moves along a straight railroad track. If its position is given by $s = 8t^3 - 12t^2 + 6t - 1$ with s in miles and t in hours, what distance does it travel from $t = 0$ to $t = 1$?

Answer: 2 miles.

Explanation: Plug in $t = 0$ and $t = 1$. Distance $= |-1-1| = 2$.

89) Compute $\int \sec^2 x\,dx$

Answer: $\tan x + C$

90) Compute $\int \csc^2 x\, dx$

Answer: $-\cot x + C$

91) Compute $\int \cos 3x\, dx$

Answer: $\dfrac{1}{3}\sin 3x + C$

92) Compute $\int (x-2)^{3/2}\, dx$

Answer: $\dfrac{2}{5}(x-2)^{5/2} + C$

93) Compute $\int (2x^2+3)^{1/3} x\, dx$

Answer: $\dfrac{3}{16}(2x^2+3)^{4/3} + C$

94) Compute $\int_0^2 10x^2 + 10\, dx$

Answer: $\dfrac{140}{3}$

Explanation: $\int_0^2 10x^2 + 10\, dx = 10\int_0^2 x^2 + 1\, dx = 10\left(\dfrac{14}{3}\right) = \dfrac{140}{3}$

95) Compute $\int \dfrac{dx}{\sin^2 x}$

Answer: $-\cot x$

96) Compute $\int_{-3}^{-1}(\frac{1}{x^2}-\frac{1}{x^3})dx$

Answer: $\frac{10}{9}$

97) Compute $\int_{-3}^{3}\sin\frac{x}{5}dx$

Answer: 0

98) Computer $\int_{-2}^{2}(x^3-x^5)dx$

Answer: 0

99) Compute $\int_{-\pi/2}^{\pi/2}\cos x\,dx$

Answer: 2

100) The number of bacteria in a culture grows exponentially with a growth constant equal to 0.02. Initially, there are 1,000 bacteria present. How many bacteria will be present after 1 hour?

Answer: 1020 bacteria

Explanation: Use the exponential growth/decay equation.
$y = 1000e^{0.02} = 1020.2 \approx 1020$ bacteria

Limits

(5 Questions)

For questions 1-3 consider the following graph of $f(x)$:

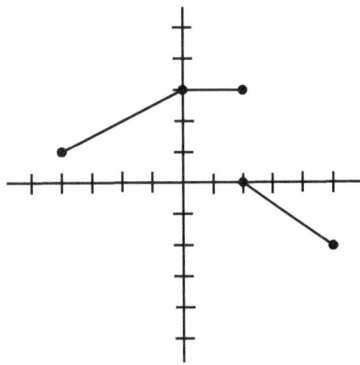

101) Determine $\lim_{x \to -2} f(x)$

   A) 2
   B) 3
   C) 0
   D) ∞
   E) Does not exist

102) Determine $\lim_{x \to 2} f(x)$

   A) 2
   B) 3
   C) 0
   D) ∞
   E) Does not exist

103) Determine $\lim_{x \to 0} f(x)$

   A) 2
   B) 3
   C) 0
   D) ∞
   E) Does not exist

104) $\lim\limits_{x \to 0} \dfrac{\sin^3 x + \sin x \cos^2 x}{x} = ?$

   A) 0
   B) 2
   C) $\dfrac{\pi}{2}$
   D) π
   E) Does not exist

105) $\lim\limits_{x \to \frac{3\pi}{2}^+} \sec x$

   A) 1
   B) -1
   C) ∞
   D) $-\infty$
   E) Does not exist

Differential Calculus
(25 Questions)

106) Find the instantaneous rate of change of $x^2 + 2x + 1$ at $x = 2$ using the definition of a derivative.

   A) 1
   B) 2
   C) 6
   D) 10
   E) None of the above

107) Find the instantaneous rate of change of $12x + 1$ at $x = 6$ using the definition of a derivative.

   A) 1
   B) 2
   C) 6
   D) 12
   E) 13

108) If $f(x) = \dfrac{x^3}{3} + 4x^2 + 1$ find $f'(x)$

   A) $x^2 + 2x$
   B) $x^2 + 16x + 1$
   C) $x^2 + 8x$
   D) $2x^3 + 6x^2 + x$
   E) $\dfrac{2}{3}x^2 + 2x$

109) Find the derivative of $f(x) = \ln(4x) + \sin(3x^2)$

   A) $\dfrac{6\cos(3x^2)}{x}$
   B) $\dfrac{1}{4x} + 6x\sin(3x^2)$
   C) $\dfrac{1}{x} + 6x\cos(3x^2)$
   D) $\dfrac{4}{x} + 6x\cos(3x^2)$
   E) 1

110) $\dfrac{d}{dx}\left(\sin(4x^2)\cos(3x)\right)$

   A) $-3\sin(4x^2)\sin(3x) + 8x\cos(4x^2)\cos(3x)$
   B) $3\sin(4x^2)\sin(3x) - 8x\cos(4x^2)\cos(3x)$
   C) $8x\sin(4x^2)\sin(3x) - 3\cos(4x^2)\cos(3x)$
   D) $-24x^2\sin^2(4x^2)\sin^2(3x)$
   E) $-3\sin(12x^3) + 8x\cos(12x^3)$

111) $\dfrac{d}{dx}\left(\dfrac{1}{\ln(4x+1)}\right) = ?$

   A) $\dfrac{-4}{\ln^2(4x+1)}$
   B) $\dfrac{-4}{4x\ln(4x+1)}$
   C) $\dfrac{-4(4x+1)}{\ln(4x+1)}$
   D) $-16x + \ln(4x+1)$
   E) $\dfrac{-4}{(4x+1)\ln^2(4x+1)}$

112) $\dfrac{d}{dx}\left(2e^{3x}\right)$

A) $6xe^{3x}$
B) $6e^{2x}$
C) $6xe^{2x}$
D) $6e^{3x}$
E) $6xe^{2}$

113) Consider the graph of $f(x)$

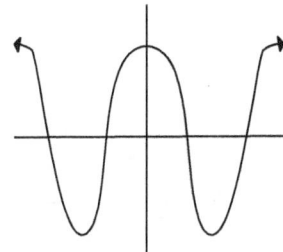

Which of the following graphs shows the corresponding $f''(x)$?

A)
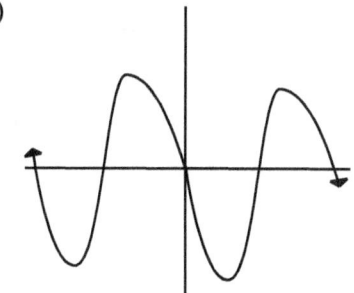

C)
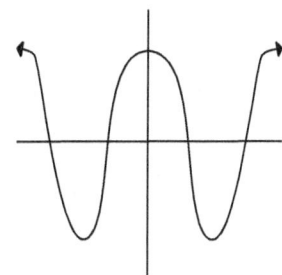

B)
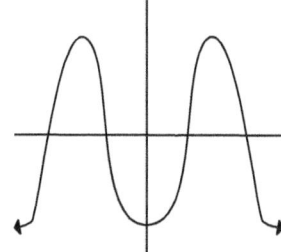

D)
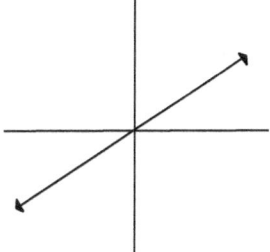

E)
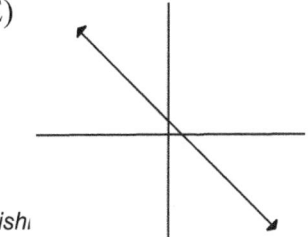

114) Consider the graph of $f''(x)$

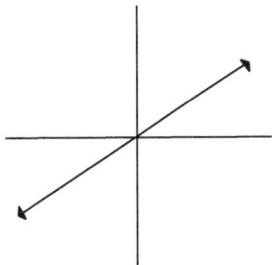

Which of the following graphs is most likely the corresponding $f(x)$?

A)

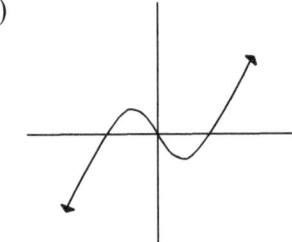

C)

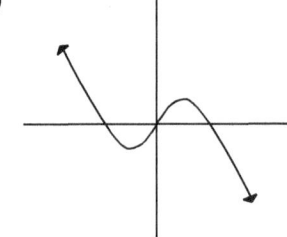

B)

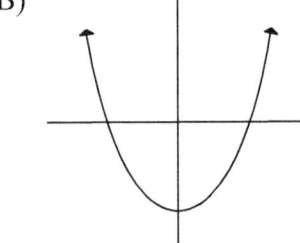

D)

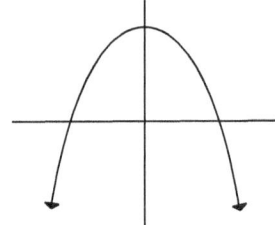

E)

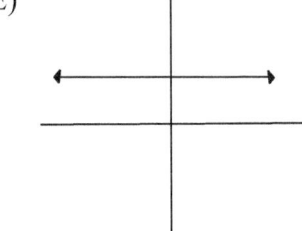

115) Use L'Hopitals rule to find $\lim\limits_{x \to 0} \dfrac{2\cos 2x - 2\cos 2x}{1 - \cos x}$

   A) 0
   B) 1
   C) 2
   D) 3
   E) 6

116) Use L'Hopitals rule to find $\lim\limits_{x \to 0} \dfrac{x^2 + 2x}{\sin x}$

   A) 0
   B) 1
   C) 2
   D) 6
   E) Does not exist

117) According to the mean value theorem for derivatives, which of the following is true?

   A) The average slope is equal to the instantaneous slope of at least one point on the interval.
   B) The instantaneous slope is equal to over half of the points on a given interval.
   C) The average slope is almost always correctly approximated using the instantaneous slope.
   D) The mean of the values on an interval will be the point at which the instantaneous slope will be most accurately calculated.
   E) None of the above

118) Which of the following is continuous but not differentiable?

A)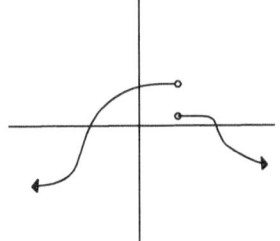

C)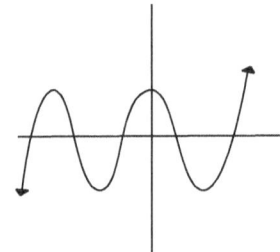

B)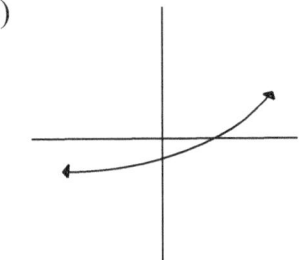

D)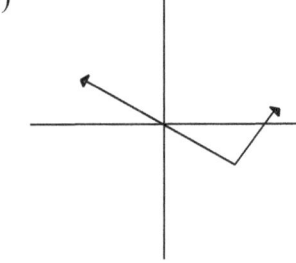

E) None of the above

119) Which of the following is not continuous or differentiable?

A)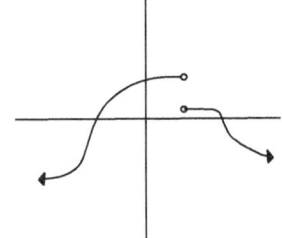

C)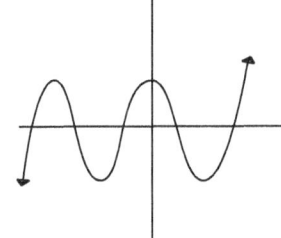

B)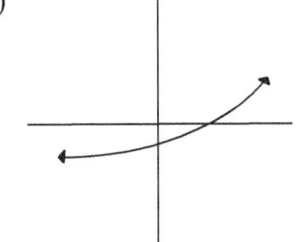

D)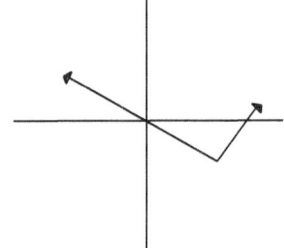

E) None of the above

120) The position of a particle varies according to the function $f(x) = x^3 - 2x^2 + x + 1$. How many times does the particle change direction?

A) 0
B) 1
C) 2
D) 3
E) 4

121) Suppose that the temperature in a given room during the hours between 6:00 AM and 6:00 PM varies according to the function $f(t) = 4t^2 - 16t + 60$. At what time of day will the house be the coolest and what temperature will it be? (Consider 6:00 AM to be hour 1)

A) 6:00, 44 degrees
B) 8:00, 44 degrees
C) 8:00, 48 degrees
D) 7:00, 44 degrees
E) 6:00, 48 degrees

122) The position of a car going down the road changes according to the function $f(t) = 2t^3 - t^2 + 6t + 1$. Which of the following equations describes the car's acceleration?

A) $a(t) = 12t^2 + 2$
B) $a(t) = 6t^2 - 2t + 6$
C) $a(t) = 6t^2 + 2t$
D) $a(t) = 12$
E) $a(t) = 12t - 2$

123) The position of a particle varies according to the function $f(t) = t^4 - 3t^3 + 2t^2 + t + 1$. At what time will the car's acceleration be at a minimum?

A) $t = 0$
B) $t = .75$
C) $t = 1.2$
D) $t = 2$
E) $t = 6$

124) Consider the graph of $f(x) = x^3 + x^2 + x + 1$. At how many points does the concavity change?

   A) 0
   B) 1
   C) 2
   D) 3
   E) 4

125) As an object falls toward the ground, its position changes according to the equation $f(x) = 4.9t^2 + 3t + 7$. What is the object's initial velocity?

   A) 4.9
   B) 9.8
   C) 7
   D) 3
   E) 0

126) A cylindrical silo of radius 5 feet is filled with oats at a rate of 400 cubic feet per minute. At approximately what rate does the depth of the oats in the silo change?

   A) 2 ft/min
   B) 4 ft/min
   C) 6 ft/min
   D) 8 ft/min
   E) 10 ft/min

127) A balloon is filled with air at a rate of 3 cubic inches per second. At what rate is the diameter changing when the radius is 4 inches?

   A) .04 in/sec
   B) .09 in/sec
   C) 1.2 in/sec
   D) 3 in/sec
   E) None of the above

128) A cylindrical object is being filled with water at a rate of 2 cubic inches per second. As it is filled, the object keeps its cylindrical shape though its size increases. The radius remains constant while the height changes. What rate (in inches per second) is the cylinders height changing at if its radius is 1 inch?

A) $\dfrac{2}{\pi}$

B) $\dfrac{\pi}{2}$

C) $\dfrac{1}{\pi^2}$

D) $\dfrac{1}{2}$

E) $\dfrac{\pi}{3}$

129) Find the equation of the line tangent to $f(x) = x^3 + 2x^2 + 3$ at $x = 3$

A) $L(x) = 33x - 10$
B) $L(x) = 3x - 51$
C) $L(x) = 3.1x - 15$
D) $L(x) = x^3 + 2x^2 + 3$
E) $L(x) = 39x - 69$

130) Find the derivative of $\dfrac{\sin x + 2}{3x}$

A) $\dfrac{3x\cos x + 3\sin x + 2}{3x^2}$

B) $\dfrac{x\cos x - \sin x - 2}{3x^2}$

C) $\dfrac{3x\cos x + 3\sin x + 6}{3x^2}$

D) $\dfrac{x\cos x + \sin x + 3}{3x\sin x}$

E) None of the above

Integral Calculus
(20 Questions)

131) $\int (x^2 + 3x + 1)dx = ?$

  A) $\dfrac{x^3}{2} + \dfrac{x^2}{2} + 2x + C$

  B) $2x + 3$

  C) $x^3 + \dfrac{x^2}{3} + 2x + C$

  D) $\dfrac{x^3}{3} + \dfrac{3x^2}{2} + x + C$

  E) $\dfrac{x^3 + x^2}{6} + 2x + C$

132) $\int \dfrac{dx}{3x + 2} = ?$

  A) $\ln(3x + 2) + C$
  B) $3\ln(3x + 2) + C$
  C) $\dfrac{-1}{(3x + 2)} + C$
  D) $\dfrac{\ln(3x)}{(3x + 2)} + C$
  E) $\dfrac{\ln(3x + 2)}{3} + C$

133) $\int e^{2x} dx$

  A) $\dfrac{1}{2}e^{2x} + C$
  B) $2e^{2x} + C$
  C) $\dfrac{e^x}{2} + C$
  D) $2e^x + C$
  E) None of the above

134) $\int \dfrac{3x+4}{x^2+5x+6} dx = ?$

   A) $(3x+4)\ln(x^2+5x+6)+C$
   B) $\dfrac{\ln(x^2+5x+6)}{3}+C$
   C) $-2\ln(x+2)+5\ln(x+3)+C$
   D) $-2\ln(x+3)+5\ln(x+2)+C$
   E) Cannot be solved

135) $\int \dfrac{1}{x^2+25} dx$

   A) $5\tan^{-1} x + C$
   B) $5\tan^{-1} \dfrac{x}{25} + C$
   C) $\dfrac{-1}{(x+5)^2} + C$
   D) $\dfrac{1}{5}\tan^{-1} \dfrac{x}{5} + C$
   E) Cannot be solved

136) A particle starts from rest at time $t = 0$ and its velocity follows the equation $v(t) = \dfrac{1}{4}t^2 + 3t + 7$. How far does the particle travel in the first three seconds?

   A) 15.4
   B) 19.2
   C) 21.5
   D) 29.6
   E) 36.8

137) A baseball is released from an air balloon. Gravity takes hold of it and causes it to accelerate at a rate of 9.8 m/s. How far has it fallen after 12 seconds?

   A) 100 m
   B) 356 m
   C) 540 m
   D) 705 m
   E) 800 m

138) A projectile is launched directly upward and gravity takes hold of it and causes it to decelerate at a rate of approximately 10 m/s. If it was initial launched at a velocity of 100 m/s, how far will it have traveled when gravity causes it to come to a rest?

A) 300 m
B) 420 m
C) 510 m
D) 640 m
E) 700 m

139) Find the area from $x = 0$ to $x = 4$ bounded by $f(x) = 2x +$ and the x-axis below using Reimann Sums with a left endpoint approximation and a base 1.

A) 16
B) 18
C) 20
D) 22
E) 24

140) Find the area from $x = 0$ to $x = 4$ bounded by $f(x) = 2x +$ and the x-axis below using Reimann Sums with a right endpoint approximation and a base 1.

A) 16
B) 18
C) 20
D) 22
E) 24

141) Find the integral of the graph below from $x = 0$ to $x = 10$

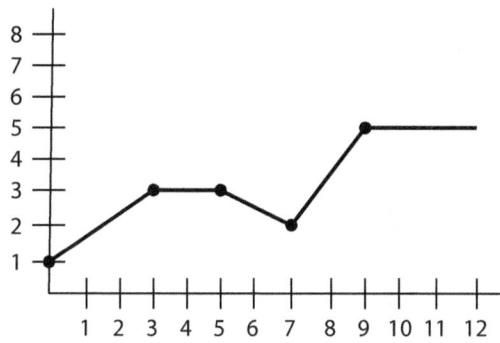

A) 12
B) 16
C) 27
D) 29
E) Cannot be found without more information

142) Find the area bounded by the two curves and y-axis as shown below.

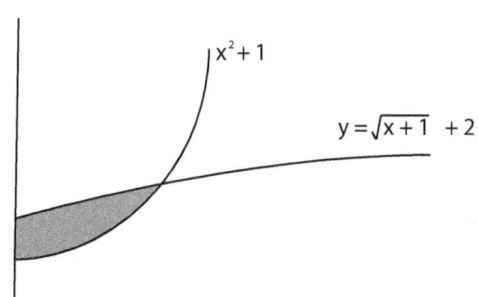

A) 2.661
B) 3.03
C) 3.128
D) 3.446
E) 4

143) Find the area bounded by the x-axis, y-axis and two curves as shown below.

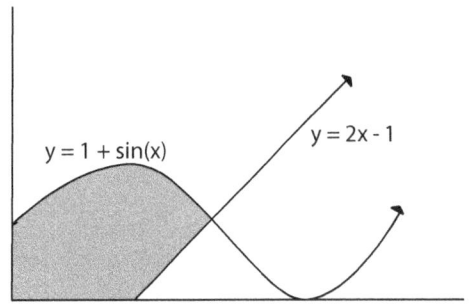

A) 1.332
B) 1.057
C) 2.013
D) 1.965
E) 2.227

144) Find the area bounded by the three lines as shown below.

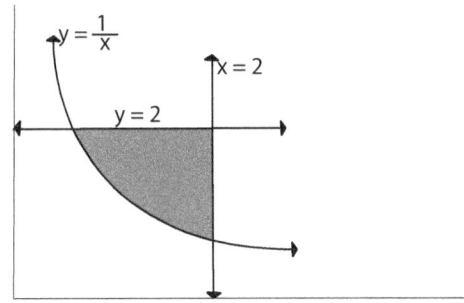

A) 1.443
B) 1.726
C) 2.015
D) 1.546
E) 1.614

145) Find the average value of $f(x) = x^3 + 2x^2 - 3$ over the interval [4,7].

A) 189.12
B) 198.67
C) 237.75
D) 465.38
E) 713.25

146) Find the volume of the area bounded by $f(x) = -(x-1)^2 +$ and the x-axis when rotated about the x-axis.

A) 2π
B) 2.4π
C) 3.12π
D) 3.7π
E) 9.3

147) Which of the following is a correct statement of the Fundamental Theorem?

A) $\int_a^b F(x)dx = F(a) - F(b)$

B) $\int_a^b F(x)dx = F(b)F(a)$

C) $\dfrac{d}{dx}\int_a^x f(t) = f(t)$

D) $\int_a^b F'(x)dx = F(b) - F(a)$

E) $\dfrac{d}{dx}\int_x^y f(t) = f(y-x)$

148) Find the volume of the area bounded by $y = \sqrt{2x-6}$, $x = 5$ and the x-axis when rotated about the y-axis

A) 22.4π
B) 30π
C) 16π
D) 18.9π
E) 40π

149) A factory has a machine which produces wind up toys at a rate which follows the equation $f(h) = h^3 + 3h + \dfrac{1}{h}$. How many toys would the machine complete in the first four hours of production?

A) 70
B) 89
C) 74
D) 82
E) 97

150) A certain interstate has off ramps spaced apart such that they follow the equation $f(x) = 4x^2 + 3x + 1$. How many off ramps would a person pass in the first five miles of the interstate?

A) 210
B) 156
C) 98
D) 74
E) 50

Answer Key

101)	A	127)	A
102)	E	128)	A
103)	B	129)	E
104)	B	130)	B
105)	C	131)	D
106)	C	132)	E
107)	D	133)	A
108)	C	134)	C
109)	C	135)	D
110)	A	136)	E
111)	E	137)	D
112)	D	138)	C
113)	B	139)	A
114)	A	140)	E
115)	A	141)	D
116)	C	142)	B
117)	A	143)	A
118)	D	144)	E
119)	A	145)	C
120)	C	146)	B
121)	B	147)	D
122)	E	148)	A
123)	B	149)	B
124)	B	150)	A
125)	D		
126)	C		

 Test-Taking Strategies

Here are some test-taking strategies that are specific to this test and to other CLEP tests in general:
- Keep your eyes on the time. Pay attention to how much time you have left.
- Read the entire question and read all the answers. Many questions are not as hard to answer as they may seem. Sometimes, a difficult sounding question really only is asking you how to read an accompanying chart. Chart and graph questions are on most CLEP tests and should be an easy free point.
- If you don't know the answer immediately, the new computer-based testing lets you mark questions and come back to them later if you have time.
- Read the wording carefully. Some words can give you hints to the right answer. There are no exceptions to an answer when there are words in the question such as always, all or none. If one of the answer choices includes most or some of the right answers, but not all, then that is not the correct answer. Here is an example:

    The primary colors include all of the following:

    A) Red, Yellow, Blue, Green
    B) Red, Green, Yellow
    C) Red, Orange, Yellow
    D) Red, Yellow, Blue
    E) None of the above

    Although item A includes all the right answers, it also includes an incorrect answer, making it incorrect. If you didn't read it carefully, were in a hurry, or didn't know the material well, you might fall for this.
- Make a guess on a question that you do not know the answer to. There is no penalty for an incorrect answer. Eliminate the answer choices that you know are incorrect. For example, this will let your guess be a 1 in 3 chance instead.

 What Your Score Means

Based on your score, you may, or may not, qualify for credit at your specific institution. At University of Phoenix, a score of 50 is passing for full credit. At Utah Valley University, the score is unpublished, the school will accept credit on a case-by-case basis. Another school, Brigham Young University (BYU) does not accept CLEP credit. To find out what score you need for credit, you need to get that information from your school's website or academic advisor.

You can score between 20 and 80 on any CLEP test. Some exams include percentile ranks. Each correct answer is worth one point. You lose no points for unanswered or incorrect questions.

 Test Preparation

How much you need to study depends on your knowledge of a subject area. If you are interested in literature, took it in school, or enjoy reading then your studying and preparation for the literature or humanities test will not need to be as intensive as someone who is new to literature.

This book is much different than the regular CLEP study guides. This book actually teaches you the information that you need to know to pass the test. If you are particularly interested in an area, or feel like you want more information, do a quick search online. There is a lot you'll need to memorize. Almost everything in this book will be on the test. It is important to understand all major theories and concepts listed in the table of contents. It is also very important to know any bolded words.

Don't worry if you do not understand or know a lot about the area. If you study hard, you can complete and pass the test.

To prepare for the test, make a series of goals. Allot a certain amount of time to review the information you have already studied and to learn additional material. Take notes as you study-it will help you learn the material.

 Legal Note

All rights reserved. This Study Guide, Book and Flashcards are protected under US Copyright Law. No part of this book or study guide or flashcards may be reproduced, distributed or stored in a retrieval system, or transmitted in any form or by any means, electronic, mechanical, photocopying, recording, or otherwise, without the prior written permission of the publisher Breely Crush Publishing, LLC. This manual is not supported by or affiliated with the College Board, creators of the CLEP test. CLEP is a registered trademark of the College Entrance Examination Board, which does not endorse this book.

FLASHCARDS

This section contains flashcards for you to use to further your understanding of the material and test yourself on important concepts, names or dates. Read the term or question then flip the page over to check the answer on the back. Keep in mind that this information may not be covered in the text of the study guide. Take your time to study the flashcards, you will need to know and understand these concepts to pass the test.

Derivative	Algebraic expression
Ellipse	Hyperbola
What is De L'Hopital's rule?	Terms
Coefficient of the variable	Polynomial

Collection of terms that are separated by arithmetic operations	A derivative of a function represents the rate of change of the function
Look like two parabolas that are reflected over a line of symmetry	Locus of all points in a plane such as the sum of the distances between two fixed points
Numbers and variables	De L'Hopital's rule enables you to calculate limits of ratios of functions, when both a numerator and denominator approach either zero or infinity
Expression containing the sum of a finite number of terms	The number multiplied by the variable

FOIL	Factor
Simplify	Antiderivatives
Balance in equations	Quadratic equation
What is the solution to a quadratic equation?	Vertex

Two numbers or terms that when multiplied together yield the original term	First, out, inner, last
The opposite of derivatives	Solve or reduce
One variable is an equation that can be changed into the form $ax^2+bx+c=0$	The value of each side of the equation is the same
The lowest point on the parabola	The root of the polynomial $ax^2+bx+c=0$

In graphing the term x runs horizontal or vertical?	In graphing the term y runs horizontal or vertical?
What is absolute value?	| |
≠	≤
≥	<

Vertical	Horizontal
Notation for absolute value	The distance between a number and 0 on the number line
Notation for less than or equal to	Notation for not equal to
Notation for less than	Notation for greater than or equal to

>	Parallel lines
Perpendicular lines	⊥
Another term for an antiderivative	Logarithms
Natural logarithms	When are logarithms and exponents used?

Two lines are parallel if the lie on the same plane and never intersect	Notation for greater than
Notation for perpendicular	Two lines are perpendicular if their intersection forms a right angle
The exponent of a positive number	Integral
To calculate simple & compound interest and exponential growth	Have a base "e" which is a constant

Radius	Diameter
Chord	Central Angle
Arc	Major arc
{ }	Another name for empty set

Diameter of a circle is twice the radius	A line segment joining the center to a point on the circle
Formed by two radii	A line that goes through the center of the circle
An arc that is greater than a semicircle	Continuous part of the circle
Null set	Empty set

Algebraic equation	$\|\ \|$
Constant of integration	What are related rates of change?
What is continuity?	What are derivatives of higher order?
What is the relation between differentiability and continuity?	How do you find the slope at a point in Calculus?

Notation for parallel	Must contain an equal sign
Related rates of change deal with two parameters that affect each other	"C"
The derivative of a function f(x) is f'(x) which is called the first derivative. Successive derivatives of f(x) are higher order derivatives.	A function f(x) is continuous if it is continuous at every point of its domain
It is the slope of the tangent line to that graph at the point	If a function is differentiable at some point then it is a continuous function at this point

NOTES

NOTES

NOTES

NOTES

NOTES

NOTES

NOTES

NOTES

NOTES

NOTES

NOTES

NOTES

NOTES

NOTES

NOTES

NOTES

NOTES

NOTES

NOTES

NOTES

NOTES

NOTES

NOTES

NOTES

NOTES

NOTES

NOTES

NOTES

NOTES

NOTES

NOTES

NOTES

NOTES

NOTES

NOTES

NOTES

NOTES

NOTES

NOTES

NOTES

www.ingramcontent.com/pod-product-compliance
Lightning Source LLC
Chambersburg PA
CBHW081832300426
44116CB00014B/2561